Zhang Heng Counted Stars

Zhang Heng (A.D. 78-139), a famous scientist of ancient China, was once made a court official in charge of the astronomy work of the Eastern Han (A.D. 25-220). He was proficient in calendar-making and invented the armillary sphere, a model of the heavens, and the seismograph to record earthquakes. He was also the first to find out the cause of the lunar eclipse.

The Chinese ancestors had three theories of the composition and motion of the universe which were as follows:

The sky is like a round canopy which revolves counterclockwise, and the sun, the moon and the stars revolve clockwise; the earth is a square with each side being 400,000 kilometres....

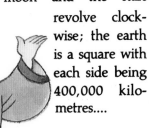

The sky has no shape and the sun, the moon and the stars all float in the sky.

The sky is like an egg shell and the earth the yolk. They float above the air and revolve constantly.

1

2

Science Stories of Ancient China

Stories of Scientists in Ancient China

Zhang Heng Counted Stars
Zu Chongzhi and the Value of π
Yi Xing Revised Calendars
Traveller Xu Xiake

DOLPHIN BOOKS

图书在版编目（CIP）数据

中国古代科学家 / 朱抗编写; 洪涛, 冯聪英绘.
北京: 海豚出版社, 2005. 7
（中国古代科学故事丛书）
ISBN 7-80138-495-4

I. 中... II. ①朱...②洪...③冯...
III. 科学家－列传－中国－古代－英文
IV. K826. 1

中国版本图书馆CIP数据核字（2005）第080906号

First Edition 2005

ISBN 7-80138-495-4

© Dolphin Books, Beijing, 2005

Published by Dolphin Books
24 Baiwanzhuang Road, Beijing 100037, China

Distributed by China International Book Trading
Corporation
35 Chegongzhuang Xilu, Beijing 100044, China
P.O.Box 399, Beijing, China

Printed in the People's Republic of China

3

4

In A.D. 117 Zhang Heng completed the first bronze celestial globe, or armillary sphere, generated by waterpower in the world. It can show people the laws of motion of the sun, the moon and the stars.

Your Majesty, the outer girth of the armillary sphere is about 4.87 meters and is divided into 365¼ degrees. It rotates from the Winter Solstice this year to next year's, with one cycle a year.

Above is the schematic diagram of the movement of the globe as recorded in an ancient book. Zhang Heng used the force of the water drops to move the armillary sphere slowly, in accordance with time so as to demonstrate the motion, namely fullness and wane, of the moon.

The revolving armillary sphere demonstrates the celestial phenomena of the four seasons and the twelve two-hour periods.

How come it can revolve?

Your Majesty, the dripping water moves the big wheel, which drives the small one, so as to make the armillary sphere rotate slowly.

I'd like to see it myself tonight.

Ah! The stars in the sky really do correspond to the constellation on the armillary sphere.

After years of research and observation Zhang Heng wrote *Ling Xian* (*The Spiritual Constitution of the Universe*) and *Hun Tian Yi Tu Zhu* (*The Diagrams of the Armillary Sphere*) and became known as the famous astronomer of the mid-Eastern Han Dynasty.

One day Zhang Heng and his family were drinking and admiring the full moon from a pavillion.

There were 26 quite strong earthquakes between A.D. 92 and 125. Zhang Heng recorded the conditions of the earthquakes.

8

The seismograph was completed in A.D. 132.

Right. They are east, south, west, north, northwest, southwest, northeast and southeast. No matter in which direction the earthquake takes place, the ball in that direction will fall out of the dragon's mouth into the frog's mouth.

Father, do the eight dragons indicate eight directions?

Let me vibrate it!

I'm so tired!

Your vibration is too slight for a ball to fall.

a. The inside of the seismograph has been lost. According to *Hou Han Shu* (*History of the Later Han Dynasty*) · *Biography of Zhang Heng*, people figured out the structural fundamentals of the seismograph as follows:

Zhang Heng lived to be sixty-two. He made many outstanding inventions and contributions in his life.

b. There is a heavy stick in the centre of the seismograph. The upper part of the stick is bigger than the lower part.

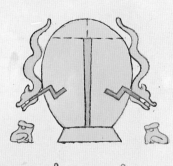

c. As long as there is an earthquake, the stick will fall to the direction where the earthquake takes place.

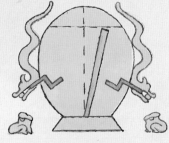

Here is a bronze bird wind director, with its head always pointing to the wind direction and its body always revolving in accordance with the wind-force. This is the earliest anemoscope or wind metre in Chinese history.

d. The fallen stick hits the crooked rod and the rod opens the dragon mouth, then the bronze ball falls into the frog's mouth.

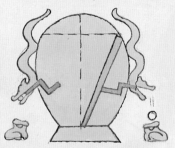

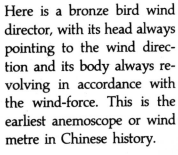

Zhang Heng made a drum cart for mileage-recording based on the principle of gears. For every one *li* (one *li* equals 500 m.) the cart goes forward the wooden figurine will beat the drum once. For every ten *li* the cart goes forward the wooden figurine will beat the clock once.

Zhang Heng also excelled in arithmetic and he figured out the value of π as 3.1622

Zhang Heng was also a famous writer and his *Ode to the Two Capitals*, *Ode to the Tillers* and *Four Laments* were very popular in the literary circles of his time.

Zhang Heng was also one of the four great painters of the Eastern Han Dynasty.

His tomb is at his home town, Nanyang, Henan.

Zu Chongzhi and the Value of π

Zu Chongzhi (A.D. 429-500) was a scientist of the Southern Dynasties. He discovered the real value of π lay between the two numbers, 3.1415926 and 3.1415927, and also gave two fractional values for π: an "inaccurate value" (yuelü) 22/7 , and an "accurate value" (milü) 355/113 . He also excelled in astronomy and invented the Daming Calendar.

Zu Chongzhi's grandfather was an imperial official in charge of construction engineering and often went to inspect the construction sites.

Father, don't overwork.

Thank you. I can manage.

Grandpa, it's so stuffy....

Chongzhi, where are you? Stop!

This was *Ling Xian* (*The Spiritual Constitution of the Universe*) written by Zhang Heng, astronomer of the Eastern Han Dynasty. The ten-year-old Zu Chongzhi read it with great interest. A new world opened before him.

What are you doing?

I'm trying to understand the waxing and waning of the moon.

Seeing his grandson becoming infatuated with astronomy, the grandfather took him to visit scholar He Chengtian.

Your Excellency, my grandson wants to be your student.

Grandpa He, please accept my respects.

All right.

What's the use of erecting a bamboo pole here?

This is called an "earth sundial" and is used to locate the position of the sun in the sky.

.Look, the shadow of the pole is a little over one chi in summer and more than ten chi in winter. I've kept the records for several years, so that I can tell the season and the time of the day by looking at the shadow of the pole.

Yesterday's shadow was the longest, so it should be the Winter Solstice. Why does the calendar say the day after tomorrow will be the Winter Solstice?

Good question! What I want to do is to make a new calendar.

Since then Zu Chongzhi became the student of He Chengtian. Together with his teacher, he observed the heavenly bodies and noted down their observations, thereby making a systematic study of astronomy, calendar and mathematics. Not long after the Yuanjia Calendar made by He Chengtian was published.

At the age of 25, Zu entered the Hualin Academic Institution, an imperial body for advanced learning.

On September 15, A.D. 459, Zu forecast that there would be a lunar eclipse....

Chinese people hadn't mastered written calculation or calculation with an abacus at that time, so Zu used these small sticks to calculate the celestial phenomena.

In A.D. 462 Zu completed the Daming Calendar which improved the method of measuring lunar years and adopted the year difference.

17

Emperor Xiaowu called in the ministers to discuss the publishing of the Daming Calendar.

In A.D. 464 emperor Xiaowu died and the adoption of the new calendar was laid aside. Zu was dismissed from office and went home.

The value of π means the ratio of the circumference of a circle to its diameter. There is a theory that "If the diameter is 1, the circumference will be 3" in ancient China, but it is incorrect.

In order to meet the needs of construction engineering, machine building, container improving, calendar making and astronomy, the ancient mathematicians gave their own values for π.

Left: Liu Xin of the Western Han Dynasty
Right: Zhang Heng of the Eastern Han Dynasty

In the late period of the third century Liu Hui, a mathematician, calculated π value by cutting the area of the circle into segments.

Your Excellency, you've been observing me cutting stones for several days. Have you learnt anything?

Yes, I've learnt a lot!

Let me measure i The circumference a hexagon is just three times its diametre!

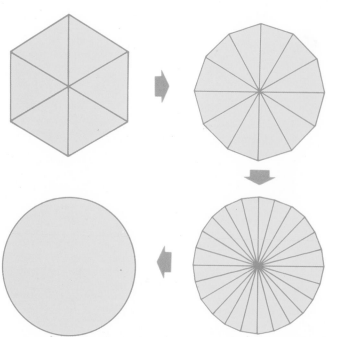

The mason cuts off the segments of the hexagon stone, making it a dodecagon; then he cuts off the segments of the dodecagon, making it a twenty-four sided polygon. The exact circle is obtained when the segments so cut off become infinitesimals.

As the number of sides of the polygon increases, its circumference become increasingly closer to tha of the circle. Let me calculate this....

Through this method, Liu H worked out that the circumfe ence of a 192-side polygon w. 157/50 of its diameter, or 3.1 times.

Zu was much inspired by Liu's way of calculating by cutting off the segments of the circle.

Don't hurry. Draw an exact circle!

Fine. Good idea.

Dad, we'll cut more segments off the circle than Liu did.

I've cut 192 segments.

It's 3.14 exactly! What a marvelous job Liu Hui did!

Numerous days passed, numerous circles were drawn and numerous segments were cut off. Finally, Zu calculated the value of π as being between 3.1415926 and 3.1415927. He was the first person in the world to give such an accurate value for π.

Zu was versatile. He excelled in machine building, literature and music. He once rebuilt the south-pointing cart which had been lost during his time. He also created the methods of husking rice and milling flour by water power.

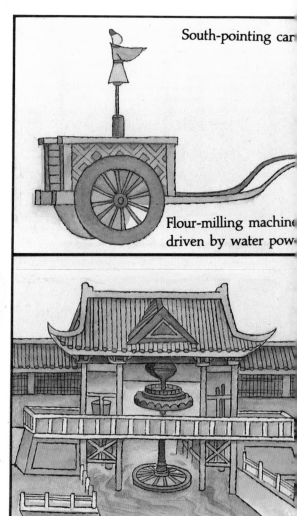

South-pointing cart

Flour-milling machine driven by water power

22

Zu died in A.D. 500. His son carried on his cause. Ten years later his Daming Calendar was published and adopted.

Yi Xing Revised Calendars

Yi Xing (A.D. 683-727), originally named Zhang Sui, was an eminent monk and astronomist of the Tang Dynasty. He made the Dayan Calendar which was used for nearly 1,000 years. He also contributed a lot to observing the heavenly bodies, making astronomical instruments, and directing astronomical and geodetic surveys.

There was a Taoist temple—Yuandu Temple—in Chang'-an, the capital of the Tang Dynasty. The temple kept tens of thousands of books inside and there also lived a learned Taoist priest named Yin Chong. Zhang Sui, a young man, often came here to ask for advice.

Teacher, I've finished reading the "Canon of Great Mystery."

You've spent only a couple of days reading this complex book. Don't be satisfied with just a smattering of it.

Being praised by Yin Chong, Zhang Sui became known all over the capital. Wu Sansi, nephew of the emperor, sent people several times to pay visits to Zhang Sui asking to make friends with him.

In order not to become entangled with Wu Sansi, Zhang Sui resolutely left Chang'an for Mount Songshan in Henan to be a monk.

After taking the tonsure, Zhang Sui was given the Buddhist name of Yi Xing. He studied astronomy, mathematics and Buddhist sutra in Henan and then in Zhejiang, and translated the *Canon of Great Sun* and many others.

In A.D. 712 Emperor Xuanzong ascended the throne. He gave imperial edicts time and again seeking worthy persons to administer the country and named Yi Xing as the one he particularly wanted.

25

Your Majesty, though I am Zhang Sui's uncle, I may not be able to persuade him to be an official at the court.

If you don't bring him back to Chang'an, I'll punish you.

He had no choice but to go to Henan quickly and took Yi Xing back to Chang'an.

According to the calendar, there was going to be a solar eclipse on a day in A.D. 721, and thus all the civil and military officials escorted Emperor Xuanzong and waited for a whole day....

26

Yi Xing, you have a good command of astronomy and calendar and may be in charge of revising the calendar.

It's necessary to rectify and record the celestial phenomena anew. Is there any instrument for observing the celestial phenomena?

Yes, there is one in the corridor of the back hall.

How can it be used? It's so rusty. Who can help me make some new instruments?

Liang Lingzan can

Please invite him here quickly.

After four years' cooperation, Yi Xing and Liang Lingzan invented a new astronomical instrument.

Your Majesty, these rings demonstrate the motion of the sun, the moon and the stars. This object contains water to keep the instrument in balance, and this is the tube for observing the celestial phenomena, called a "sighting tube."

The sun doesn't move evenly on the ecliptic. It moves quickly in winter and slowly in summer. It seems wrong that the old calendar divides a year into 24 solar terms.

People all say that the stars are fixed, but we have observed over 150 stars with this instrument and their positions have all changed. What's the reason?

This shows that the old theory is wrong and the new calendar will correct the errors.

Another astronomical instrument named a "water-operated armillary sphere" was completed. It was placed on the terrace in front of the palace for the officials to visit.

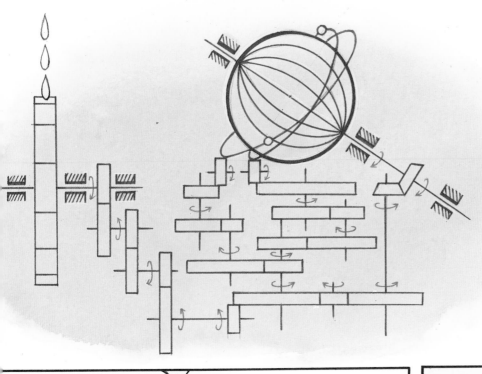

It was built on the basis of the water-operated globe made by Zhang Heng of the Eastern Han. They added two rings representing the motion of the sun and moon to the globe, which connected the driving wheels respectively. The sun ring makes an eastward circuit of the celestial globe every 365 days and the moon ring every 29 days; the globe makes a circuit backward every day. By this the motion cycle of the sun, the moon and the earth is demonstrated.

Master Yi Xing, we have accumulated considerable figures and may start to make a new calendar.

Not yet! The figures about the celestial phenomena must be verified by measurement on the spot.

The ancients say that a thousand li from north to south results in a tolerance of one cun between the shadows of bamboo poles. According to this, the earth can be easily measured.

Is this theory correct? No one has measured it. We'd better try to prove it ourselves.

In A.D. 724 a large-scale astronomical calculation began.

You go to the four counties of Henan to take measurements and please do get accurate figures.

No problem.

Yi Xing sent 12 measurement teams to all the parts of the country, with Henan as the centre. They were supposed to measure the length of the shadow of an eight-*chi*-long bamboo pole at noon in the four days of the Spring Equinox (4th solar term), Summer Solstice (10th solar term), Autumnal Equinox (16th solar term) and Winter Solstice (22nd solar term), the height of the North Pole and the exact hours of day and night.

Yi Xing calculated the meridian as 132.03 kilometres on the basis of the figures. Although a large difference compared with the modern figure of 111.2 kilometres, it was the first time man had calculated the meridian.

Yi Xing invented a special instrument for measuring the length of the meridian arc.

Based on the observation of astronomical phenomena and on-the-spot calculation, Yi Xing engrossed himself in making the new calendar—Dayan Calendar. Compared with previous ones, the Dayan Calendar had more accurate figures and was well-organized. It was one of the best calendars in ancient China, and was still in use in the sixteenth century.

Soon after the completion of the first draft of the Dayan Calendar, Yi Xing aged 45 was laid up at the Huayan Temple. He died a month later.

Traveller Xu Xiake

Xu Xiake (A.D. 1586-1641), originally named Xu Hongzu, was a geographer and traveller during the Ming Dynasty. Between the age of 22 and 56, he travelled on foot over most parts of the country and investigated and recorded various topography and landforms, leaving later generations his *Travels of Xu Xiake*.

Confucius says, "Is he not a gentleman who remains unsoured even though his merits are not recognized?"

What are you reading? Eh?

The "Illustrated Classic of Mountains and Rivers!"

You are reading such an inelegant book, instead of Confucius' works

It's a pity that the book has been confiscated.

Please tell us a story from that book!

That book tells of the world far away and says there are more than 20 kinds of barbarians....

Is there really such a strange place in the world?

Who has ever seen so many barbarians?

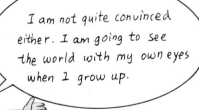

I am not quite convinced either. I am going to see the world with my own eyes when I grow up.

Xu's family had a library. Every day when he came back from school he buried himself in history books and local chronicles.

In 1607, at the age of 22 Xu Xiake got married, but he was still eager to travel.

You are going to travel. Mom has sewn a cap for you.

Thank you, Mother.

A real man should establish himself wherever he is. But, you must take care of yourself.

Yes, I know.

Come back soon, or Mother and I will worry.

Then Xu Xiake began to travel. At first he set out in spring and went home in autumn or winter, and mostly travelled to famous mountains and historical sites.

Who can see such a wonderful scene if he doesn't reach the summit?

, such a brave man!

He is Xu Xiake. As for mountain-climbing, even I can't match him.

He put up at an inn at night.

Bathe your feet in hot water, please!

No hurry. I'll write down the places I went to and scences I saw today first.

In 1613, Xu Xiake, together with his servants, came to the Yandang Mountain, Zhejiang. He marvelled at the perilous mountains and grotesque scenes here.

Such a loud sound of the waterfall! It can be heard even several li away.

Does the Dragon King spit out the water?

In the records this is called the Dalongjiu Waterfall. It starts from a lake on top of the Yandang Mountain. Let's go and find it.

37

hall we go back?

There is no foothold. Where is the lake?

Look! There may be a path under the cliff. Slip me down to the gully.

Are you kidding? You'll lose your life if you drop down!

February 1616 Xu Xiake [...] heavy snow when he [...] climbed Mount Huangshan.

Master, how can we get to the Tiandu Peak?

The snow has sealed the mountain passes and you can't get there.

We'll be careful. Please show us the way.

Go eastward along the steps. Do be careful!

The steps are covered with ice!

Too slippery!

I'll bore holes in the ice, then you just follow.

With the increase of knowledge, Xu began to probe into the inherent laws of nature and came to many scientific conclusions in his travel notes.

In 1628 Xu came to Fujian Province and made on-the-spot investigations into the Jianxi River and Ningyang River.

He wondered why the two rivers started at the same elevation but the current velocity of the Ningyang River was ten times that of the Jianxi River. By investigation, he found the reason: The Jianxi River meanders for 400 kilometres before pouring into the sea, while the Ningyang River 150 kilometres. It is the common law that the shorter the river is, the more rapid it flows.

In 1632 Xu climbed the Yandang Mountain via another path and found the lake. He discovered the lake produced two rivers indeed, but they had nothing to do with the Dalongjiu Waterfall, thus disproving previous calculations.

He was 51 years old in 1636 when he prepared for the long-distance trip to southwest China.

Dad, it's too far and you'd better not go there.

You've travelled for several decades and now may have a stable life.

I'm getting old and must make best use of my time.

Monk Jingwen was going to pay religious homage to Buddha and wanted to travel together with Xu.

Master Xu, may I travel with you?

Welcome. Come on board quickly.

Four months later the boat came to Xintang, Hunan.

Stop!

Robbers!

Run!

It's safe here. Come on!

We've lost everything. Let's go back.

You may go back. I'll go on travelling.

Me too.

43

What a grand view!

After the boat passed by Qiyang, there began to appear stone forests and stone bamboo shoots on both banks of the river. This is called "*karst* phenomenon" which results from the erosion of water on soluble limestones. Xu was the first to investigate the *karst* topography in southwest China.

44